Camping Soul Food

Recipes & Playlists

THE BUGGANS FAMILY

First Published in 2021 by Camping Soul Food
Galway, Ireland

Copyright © Malachy Duggan, Carrie Budds & Easkey Duggan, 2021

We are not professional chefs, campers or DJs, so all guidelines in this book should be taken with a pinch of salt. Please exercise caution and take responsibility when cooking outdoors.

ISBN: 978-1-911442-24-0

© Photography by Julia Dunin
www.juliadunin.com

Graphic design and editing by Amelia Walker
www.ameliadesign.net

Additional photography by the Duggan family

Printed by Modern Printers, Kilkenny, Ireland

Published with the assistance of The Manuscript Publisher
www.themanuscriptpublisher.com

Written, designed, published, printed and bound in Ireland

A CIP Catalogue record for this book is available from the National Library

To our parents,
who always supported us
when we chose the road less travelled.

Contents

Photo: **Campie, our 1990 VW T3 high top campervan**

Contents continued

Photo: **Folding camping stove toaster and locally sourced scrambled eggs**

Contents continued

*Photo: **Our trusty camping stove***

Camping Soul Food

We are the Buggans, a little family of three who love driving our campervan around Ireland. Over the last few years we've been on countless adventures, devising dishes and cooking hacks on-the-go; such as how to prepare food with limited space and storage (while the fridge keeps the beer chilled), and compiling playlists to suit every situation. Listening to brilliant tunes is even more enjoyable when you're outdoors with tasty grub and good friends.

We've put together *Camping Soul Food* with some easy recipes you can make anywhere — no-cook options, or meals you can cook on one gas ring or barbecue — and we've shared some invaluable camping hacks. Each recipe is accompanied by a music playlist to listen and dance to while you prep and cook, as well as options for alternative ingredients.

We hope you enjoy this *'recipe and hacks and soulful music'* cookbook as much as we have delighted in putting it together. We can't wait to get out in the campervan again. Meanwhile, time to stick up a tent in the garden, get out the portable stove burner, and let the imagination run wild...

Photos (from opposite): **Mal cooks up a feast; The family at Trá an Dóilin (Coral Beach)**

Meet The Buggans

Easkey Duggan *(aka Kiki, or The Boss)*

Easkey is the boss. She is currently 9 years old, going on 55. She acquired her love for the outdoors from her mother and the love of the craic from her dad. S'mores are her favourite camping food and her favourite activity is kayaking. The only thing she misses on road trips are her two cats; Annie (the ginger one) and Ella (the black one).

Carrie Budds *(aka Buggans)*

For years, Carrie has been a wanna-be surfer, a wanna-be hiker, and a wanna-be campervan queen; and now she is at least some of these things, some of the time. With a background in fitness and personal training, she is the one who sneaks vegetables and salads onto the camping dinner table, making sure the family doesn't only consume three daily meals of sausages and burgers.

Malachy Duggan *(aka The Craic)*

If Easkey is the boss, then Malachy is the brains. He has taken an innovative 'pimp my ride' approach to campervan life, festooning Campie with everything from waterproof speakers for kayaking, to a smart projector for watching movies. He loves having a beer while listening to northern soul classics, and always hangs up the hammock and sticks on the tunes before helping with the awning. He's the first to text friends to say "We're heading off this weekend. Wanna grab your tents and come along?".

Campie *(aka Campie)*

Campie is the beloved 1990 VW T3 high top campervan. Malachy and Campie have become bosom buddies (Malachy now being somewhat of an expert in 1990 VW engines, and the importance of coolant). He joined the Buggans four years ago; a fantastic addition to the family.

*Opposite: **Kiki skips before lunch;** Illustrations: **Irish Socksciety***

Photos: **Kiki enjoying Overnight Oats, Carrie hanging on a bar with Kiki, Athlone**

Egg in Toast

This is a Malachy classic that has been usurped and mastered by Kiki. If she ever makes us breakfast in bed at home, you can be guaranteed that Egg in Toast will make an appearance.

STUFF

- 1 free-range egg
- 1 slice of bread
- Cracked black pepper
- Butter
- 1 small cup

SERVES 1

METHOD OR MADNESS

1 Butter one side of bread. Place the small cup upside down on the slice and use the rim to cut a circle shaped hole.

2 Heat a non-stick frying pan over a ring or flame.

3 Fry the bread butter-side down for 40 seconds (including the removed inner circle, for dipping). Then flip over.

4 Crack the egg into toast void and fry until you reach your preferred egginess.

5 Crack fresh black pepper to serve.

MUSIC PAIRING
Roy Hamilton
*Cracking
Up Over You*

HACK

Keep an eye out for farmers selling local, fresh, and organic produce by the side of the road. Have some coins set aside for honesty boxes.

Polaroids (clockwise L-R): **Buggans & Kiki prep food outside, Lenane; Kiki in the hammock at the campsite; Egg in Toast; Kiki making marshmallow S'mores**

Huevos Rancheros

Suffering from a campfire hangover after too many beers and smoky-throated sing songs? Then this should be your go-to breakfast. Warm and hearty, it will cure what ails you.

STUFF

- 4 free-range eggs
- Handful chopped spinach
- 150ml passata
- 1 chopped red bell pepper
- 1 tbsp rapeseed oil
- 1 chopped small red chilli (optional)
- 1 chopped white onion
- 1 chopped garlic clove
- Salt and pepper
- Coriander to garnish (optional)
- 4 tortilla wraps (we prefer wholemeal)

SERVES 4

METHOD OR MADNESS

1 Put the spinach, onion, pepper, chilli, garlic, and passata into a bowl and mix thoroughly. Season with salt and pepper.

2 Heat the oil in a large pan (with a lid) over a medium heat and add the salsa mixture from Step 1.

3 Stir and cook to soften the veg.

4 Make 4 wells in the mixture and crack the eggs in these spaces.

5 Put the lid on to the pan and let the eggs cook for around 3 to 4 minutes (if the heat is not very strong, the eggs will take longer to cook).

6 Sprinkle with coriander and serve with warm tortillas on the side.

HACK

The key to cooking delicious food while camping is to be versatile and creative; necessary when you have a limited variety of ingredients to hand. Olive oil can be substituted for rapeseed oil in our recipes.

MUSIC PAIRING
Just Brothers
Sliced Tomatoes

*Photo: **Huevos Rancheros, ready to serve***

Banana Pancakes

We love, love, LOVE these pancakes. They are our choice of fuel before any run or trek as they fill you up without leaving you feeling bloated. The trick is to blitz the banana with a fork and then mix methodically with the egg until it forms a batter consistency. WARNING! they are not the same consistency as normal pancakes, but they taste delicious!

HACK

Our two main food staples when camping are eggs and bananas. They last well, come in their own biodegradable packaging and are full of fuel. If you have eggs and bananas, you have a meal!

STUFF

- **1 banana**
- **2 free-range eggs**
- **1 tsp oil (coconut oil or butter)**
- **Fruit/berries, Greek yogurt, and honey, to serve**

SERVES 1

METHOD OR MADNESS

1 Mash banana in a large bowl.

2 Whisk the eggs and then stir into the banana paste.

3 Heat the oil or butter in a large frying pan. Drop a few ladle-sized dollops of batter onto the pan, leaving room between each.

4 Fry until on each side until golden brown. Be careful when flipping the pancakes, the batter is not as cohesive as normal pancake batter.

5 Serve topped with yogurt, fresh berries, and a squeeze of honey.

♪♫
MUSIC PAIRING
Curtis Mayfield
Move On Up

Photo: **Kiki garnishing her Banana Pancakes**

Overnight Oats

One of the main reasons we love overnight oats is because they are no fuss; if you use non-dairy milk, you don't need to refrigerate the ingredients, and you can even pre-make the mix before you embark on your trip. They are nutritious, full of fibre, and will keep you full all morning. Please note that the recipe is versatile; you can substitute our suggestions with any fruit or nuts you prefer.

STUFF

INGREDIENTS

- **400ml of the milk of your choice**
- **Any fresh fruit**

PRE-MIX TO MAKE AT HOME

- **200g porridge oats**
- **1 tsp ground cinnamon**
- **50g dried fruit (raisins, chopped dates)**
- **50g nuts or seeds of choice (we love pecan nuts)**
- **2 tbsp chia seeds**

SERVES 4

METHOD OR MADNESS

PRE-MIX

- **Simply mix the ingredients together in a large jar, leaving room for the milk.**

TO MAKE UP OVERNIGHT OATS

- **The night before, mix 400ml of the milk of your choice into the premix. Seal tightly.**

- **By morning you will have a thick and creamy breakfast, ready to eat straight away. Add some berries, chopped fresh fruit, and enjoy!**

♫ ♪

MUSIC PAIRING
Frankie Valli and the Four Seasons
The Night

HACK

Pack a rope or bungee cord for your trips. Not for any specific purpose, but you'll often need one. As the sunscreen song says *"trust me on the bungee cord!"*.

Photo: **Jar of Overnight Oats**

Homemade Beans On Toast

Beans, beans are good for your heart, the more you eat, the more you... get that good protein into you! Nothing against tinned beans, but there is something so delightfully smug about making your own baked beans. And they are so tasty!

STUFF

- 1 tbsp rapeseed oil
- 1 finely diced carrot
- 1 diced celery stalk
- 400g tin haricot or cannellini beans, drained
- 2 chopped tomatoes
- 1 tsp Camping Soul Food Mix (pg. 25)
- 1 tsp Worcestershire Sauce
- Handful chopped chives (optional)
- 100ml water
- 8 wholemeal bread slices

SERVES 4

METHOD OR MADNESS

1 Heat the oil in a pan and gently cook the carrot and celery for 10 minutes until softened.

2 Add the beans, tomatoes, and *Camping Soul Food Mix,* and cook gently for a further 5 minutes until the tomatoes are softened and pulpy.

3 Stir in 100ml water and the Worcestershire sauce, cook for another 5 minutes. Cover to keep warm while the toast is on.

4 Serve each portion on two slices of wholemeal toast, topped with the chopped chives.

MUSIC PAIRING
Harold Melvin & The Blue Notes
*Wake Up Everybody (feat. **Teddy Pendergrass**)*

HACK

When making beans, always make at least double the portion. They are protein-rich, filling, and are a great option for baked potatoes. Eating them also makes you feel like a cowboy.

Photo: **Reheating Homemade Beans in an unlined tin, submerged in boiling water**

Granola

This granola recipe is another great option to make before you head off on your hollibobs. It keeps well in an airtight container. Although Malachy won't agree, there are only so many mornings you can face a full barbecued fry-up before your body says "enough"!

STUFF

- 150g nuts of choice (we love pecan, walnuts, unsalted pistachios, and blanched almonds)

- 50g dried apricots

- 100g raisins or sultanas

- 150g mixed seeds (sesame, pumpkin, flax)

- 250g porridge oats

- 1 tsp ground cinnamon

- 1 tbsp desiccated coconut (optional)

- 6 tbsps maple syrup or honey

- Zest of 1 orange

- Yogurt, fruit and berries, to serve

METHOD OR MADNESS

1 Preheat the oven to 160ºC/325ºF/ gas 3.

2 Roughly chop the nuts and apricots, then place in a large bowl. Add the remaining dry ingredients and mix together.

3 Finely grate orange zest and drizzle maple syrup into the bowl. Stir well to coat everything evenly.

4 Spread the mixture evenly over 2 large baking trays and bake in a hot oven for 20 to 25 minutes, or until golden, stirring every 10 minutes.

5 Leave to cool completely, then store in airtight jars, ready for the road. The granola will stay fresh for up to 4 weeks.

6 Serve for breakfast with natural yogurt and mixed fruit and berries of your choice.

MUSIC PAIRING
The O'Jays
Love Train

*Photo: **Kiki holding fresh fruit***

Fruit & Honey Couscous

There are occasions when you have camping visitors and you want to impress them with a delicious but healthy breakfast... this is your man! Couscous is a really handy grain for camping; it cooks quickly and is widely versatile, complimenting a variety of flavours. It is suitable for any meal, any time of the day.

STUFF

- **100g pistachios or other nuts**
- **300g couscous**
- **1/4 tsp ground cinnamon, plus more to serve**
- **8 mandarins (seedless are best)**
- **1 tsp butter**
- **1 tbsp honey**
- **300g berries**
- **500g Greek yogurt, to serve**

SERVES 4

METHOD OR MADNESS

1 Spread the nuts on a dry pan over a medium heat, toast until golden and set aside.

2 Put couscous and cinnamon into a large bowl.

3 Finely grate the zest from 2 mandarins, then squeeze their juice into a pan with the zest. Add the butter, honey, and 200ml water and bring to the boil. Pour this over the couscous, cover tightly with a lid or tin foil, then leave to absorb for 10 minutes.

4 Thinly slice the remaining mandarins.

5 Roughly chop the nuts. Fluff up the couscous with a fork, then mix the nuts through.

6 Serve the couscous in bowls, topped with the mandarins and berries.

7 Eat with a spoonful of yogurt, an extra sprinkle of cinnamon, and squeeze of honey.

MUSIC PAIRING
Gloria Jones
Tainted Love

Photo: **Campie peeking over the wall at Furbo beach**

One Cup Pancakes

This is a great recipe to make with kids, it will keep them busy for a while without making a mess. Minimising mess is important when you're working in a cramped space; whisking flour is something we strive to avoid, no one wants their bedroom/kitchen covered in a flour cloud. Tip: Use a small coffee cup for the cup measurements to avoid using scales.

STUFF

- 1 free-range egg
- 1 cup of flour (of your choice)
- 1 cup of milk (of your choice)
- Sea salt
- Oil (we love coconut oil or butter for pancakes)
- A jar with a lid

TOPPINGS

- Sweet: Berries, yogurt, honey, Nutella, lemon, and sugar
- Savoury: Ham and cheese, hummus and pesto

SERVES 4

♪♫

MUSIC PAIRING
Otis Redding
The Happy Song (Dum Dum)

METHOD OR MADNESS

1   For the batter, put the egg, flour, milk, and a pinch of sea salt into the jar. Put the lid on and shake vigorously until blended. If you have time, let the mixture rest for 30 minutes before cooking.

2   Put a frying pan on a medium heat. After a minute or so, add half a tablespoon of oil and spread evenly.

3   Add a few ladles of batter to the pan, leaving enough space between each one so they have room to spread out slightly – each ladleful will make one pancake, and you'll need to cook them in batches.

4   Cook the pancakes for 1 to 2 minutes, or until little bubbles appear on the surface and the bases are golden. Use a spatula to flip, until golden on each side.

5   Serve immediately with the toppings of your choice.

*Photo: **Flipping One Cup Pancakes***

Halloumi Breakfast Bap

We really, really love cheese. The salty, creamy, tanginess of halloumi makes it a great option for breakfast. Pair it with egg and avocado and you'll have a match made in heaven.

STUFF

- **2 baps (or Blaas if in Waterford)**
- **2 free-range eggs**
- **1 ripe avocado**
- **6 slices of halloumi cheese**
- **Fresh tomato (optional)**
- **Salt and pepper**

SERVES 2

HACK

A slotted spoon is a brilliant addition to your camping kitchen hardware. It is ideal for scooping out a perfect poached egg, but also really handy for draining food staples like pasta when you don't have a colander... or a sink!

METHOD OR MADNESS

1. **Cheese:** In a pan, on a medium heat, lightly dry fry the halloumi for 3-4 minutes.

2. **Egg:** In a pot of simmering water, create a vortex by swilling a spoon around. Drop the egg in the center of the whirlpool, then poach for 3-4 minutes (depending on how runny you like your yolk).

3. While the eggs are poaching, halve and toast the baps.

4. Mash half the avocado onto the bottom slice, or use some leftover guacamole (pg. 47).

5. Layer the remaining avocado, grilled halloumi, poached egg, and sliced tomato onto the bap. Season with salt and pepper.

6. Sandwich with the top of your bap and enjoy!

♪♫

MUSIC PAIRING
Bill Withers
Lovely Day

Photo: **Grilled halloumi and fresh tomatoes**

French Toast

While French toast makes the perfect breakfast, it can also be a brilliant option for dessert; simply by adding chocolate, fruit, cream, or anything else sweet.

STUFF

- 3 free-range eggs
- 300ml milk
- 8 slices of bread, or small bread roll halves
- 50g butter

SWEET FRENCH TOAST

- 1/3 tsp vanilla essence (optional)
- 1/2 tsp sugar (optional)

SAVOURY FRENCH TOAST

- 1/4 tsp salt
- 1/2 tsp cracked black pepper

SERVES 4

METHOD OR MADNESS

1 Beat the eggs in a shallow bowl. Add milk and sweet *or* savoury ingredients, and beat until frothy.

2 Soak each slice of bread in the egg mixture, first on one side, then the other.

3 Melt a knob of butter on a preheated frying pan on medium heat.

4 Cook both sides until golden.

5 Serve with whichever toppings you prefer. For savoury French Toast, we love cheese, bacon, mustard, sliced sausage or grilled tomato. For a sweet option, we recommend berries or fruit, honey, maple syrup, and also bacon!

HACK

Waste not, want not.
There is no need to throw away old slices of bread or bread rolls. French Toast is the perfect way to use up stale bread in a tasty way.

MUSIC PAIRING
The Dramatics
Toast To The Fool

Photo: **Kiki with a perfect honey drizzle on her French Toast**

Photos (clockwise from opposite): **Adventuring on the Wild Atlantic Way; Kiki blowing bubbles, Barna; Campie salt & pepper shakers**

Camping Soul Food Mix

You may have already gathered that, rather than qualified, experienced chefs, we are cooking enthusiasts who love travelling in our campervan, listening to class tunes, and preparing open-air feasts for ourselves and our pals. One thing that makes our culinary lives easier is to have a "ready mix" of herbs and spices that we can confidently add to many meals and be 99% sure that it will taste delicious. So far, our **Camping Soul Food Mix** hasn't let us down! We've used it in our Jambalaya, soup, as a rub for chicken... it even has its own little jar and a special place in Mal's homemade campervan kitchen unit. Now, we're not great for the old measurements but here is a best attempt at a season-all option that will steer you right when you're cooking on the fly, so you can relax and enjoy your beer instead of measuring out teaspoons of herbs and spices!

STUFF

- 1/2 tbsp cayenne pepper
- 2 tbsp smoked paprika
- 1 tbsp ground cumin
- 1 tbsp garlic powder or garlic granules
- 1/2 tbsp ground coriander
- 1 heaped tbsp dried oregano

MAKES 1 SMALL JAR

METHOD OR MADNESS

- Simply mix all the ingredients in a jar with an airtight seal and use generously.

HACK

The cayenne pepper gives this mix a bit of heat, but it's not enough to keep you warm on a damp evening out in the open. Even if you're camping in the height of summer, pack a couple of woolly hats; perfect for a chilly night, and also for bad hair days.

MUSIC PAIRING
Arthur Conley
Sweet Soul Music

*Photo: **A jar of Camping Soul Food Mix** — our reliable, go-to spice seasoning*

Barbecue Corn & Asparagus

It is great to have sides that are simple to make. We have quite a few veggie friends, so a few years ago Malachy picked up a barbecue pan; a large frying pan with lots of holes, perfect for keeping the vegetables separate from the meat. Corn and asparagus are brilliant barbecue-friendly veg options, they don't suffer too much over the heat.

STUFF

- 1 lime, zested and juiced
- 1 small red chilli
- Olive oil
- 4 corn cobs
- 1 spring onion, finely chopped
- 2 bunches asparagus, trimmed

HACK

We were given this great hack by a well-known chef. Instead of trimming asparagus, simply hold the stalk firmly on both sides of the woody end. Bend to snap. It will naturally break at the perfect spot. It's a great job for kids as it doesn't involve knives.

METHOD OR MADNESS

1 In a bowl, combine the lime zest, half of the chili (seeded and finely chopped), and 3 teaspoons of olive oil. Brush the mixture over the corn cobs (husks and silks removed, if needed) and wrap in tinfoil.

2 In another small bowl, combine half the lime juice, spring onions, remaining chilli, and a tablespoon of olive oil. Set aside.

3 Place your barbecue pan on a preheated barbecue and cook the corn for 8-10 minutes, turning regularly (remove the foil for the last few minutes to char the outside).

4 Meanwhile, rub the asparagus tips with a little oil and cook on the pan for 2-3 minutes until slightly charred and just tender.

5 Place on a serving plate and drizzle with chilli-lime dressing.

SERVES 4

♫♪ MUSIC PAIRING
The Mar-Keys
About Noon

Photo: **Veggies from the BBQ; corn and asparagus**

Bacon & Potato Salad

This is a great lunch recipe if you have some leftover potatoes from the night before. When at home, we always cook extra spuds and find the habit hard to break even on holiday. Our preferred potato for this dish is a nice, waxy baby potato with the skin on.

STUFF

- 1 tbsp mayonnaise
- Leftover potatoes (2 large, or 3 small)
- Parsley (fresh or dried)
- 2 spring onions
- 1 tsp olive oil
- 2 slices bacon (or turkey) rashers, chopped
- 1 tsp wholegrain mustard
- Salad leaves (optional)
- Cherry tomatoes, cucumber, beetroot, or any preferred salad items

SERVES 2

METHOD OR MADNESS

1 Heat a frying pan and cook the bacon or turkey in a dash of oil until crispy. Once cooked, place the bacon pieces on some kitchen paper to drain any excess oil.

2 Meanwhile, quarter the cooked potatoes (or cut into bit-sized pieces if using larger potatoes).

3 Add the bacon pieces, onion, chopped parsley, wholegrain mustard, and mayonnaise.

4 Mix well and season as required. Add the salad leaves and toss in your preferred salad items.

HACK

You are rarely more than 20 minutes away from a local shop in Ireland, and will definitely pass one before too long, even in remote areas. Don't pack for the apocalypse, and don't turn back unless you've forgotten a child... and even then...

♪♫

MUSIC PAIRING
The Blues Brothers & Aretha Franklin
Think

Photo: **Bacon & Potato Salad, perfect as a side or a main**

Cornflake Chicken Dippers

You know when you get to the end of the cereal box and all that's left are cornflake crumbs? Yes, I hate that bit too (though it is Malachy's favourite part, the weirdo!). So if you're normal like me, this is a great way to use up the crushed cereal, and if you have smaller kids it is perfect for keeping them busy and involved in the cooking process.

STUFF

- 2 small-medium chicken breasts
- 2 tbsp plain flour
- 1 tsp Camping Soul Food Mix (pg. 25)
- 1 free-range egg, beaten
- 150g cornflakes, crushed
- 2 tbsp olive oil

HACK

I've never brought weighing scales camping, so always rely on my Aunty Mag's foolproof conversion methods: a heaped tablespoon of flour equals 25g, which is an ounce, 250ml of water is approximately a small cupful.

♪♫
MUSIC PAIRING
Aretha Franklin
The Weight

METHOD OR MADNESS

1 Cut the chicken breasts into equal portions (quite thin so they will cook all the way through).

2 Mix the flour and *Camping Soul Food Mix* together, and spread onto a plate. Beat the egg in a bowl with a splash of water. Spread out the crushed cornflakes onto a separate plate.

3 This is where you can get the kids to do some of the work. Dip the chicken in the flour, next coat with the egg, then cover completely in the crushed cornflakes.

4 Heat the oil in a frying pan. Once hot, add the chicken and fry for 4-5mins each side until golden, crispy and cooked all the way through (if the chicken pieces are a bit bigger, you can pop them on the bbq or in tinfoil over the fire to cook through).

5 Serve in a wrap with salad, or with a baked potato and salsa. Whatever the kids fancy!

Photo: **Crunchy and tender Cornflake Chicken Dippers**

Spaghetti in Hot Dogs

Easkey is a fan of a YouTube channel called "5 Minute Crafts". If you've never heard of it, I definitely recommend checking it out. As well as crafts, they also have videos on camping hacks, which are both funny and useful! One day, we were watching one of their cooking hacks, and came across this dinger. Straight away we popped out to pick up a jar of hotdogs and came home to try it out. It worked fantastically. Easkey likes to eat this recipe plain — without sauce or melted cheese — but it will work perfectly coated with a marinara or cheesy sauce too.

Ideally, chop up the hotdogs (around 4 pieces per hotdog) and let the kids entertain themselves by threading hotdogs with spaghetti for as long as it takes for you to have a cuppa in peace!

STUFF

- A jar of hotdogs

- A packet of spaghetti (it has to be spaghetti)

- Optional: Pasta sauce and grated cheese

METHOD OR MADNESS

1 Cut each hotdog into about 4 pieces.

2 Push uncooked spaghetti strands through each piece of hotdog, aiming for around 3 or 4 spaghetti skewers per piece. Smaller kids might find it easier to pierce the spaghetti through the hotdog sideways, and you will get more spaghetti threads that way.

3 Add the *Spaghetti in Hot Dogs* to a pot of boiling water and cook until the pasta is tender (around 10 minutes), then drain.

4 If including cheese or a sauce, stir through, and then serve.

♪♫

MUSIC PAIRING
The Four Shells
Hot Dog

Photo: **Kiki eating her Spaghetti in Hot Dogs from the pot**

Jambalaya

The classic Jambalaya is Malachy's number one camping go-to dish when cooking for a crowd of hungry people. He has a pretty laissez-faire approach to ingredients and measurements — when we were trying to get the recipe nailed down there was a lot of "sure, a bit of this", or "sometimes I use that" — but we think we've pegged down the perfect formula now.

STUFF

- 3 chicken breasts, diced

- 8 sausages, chopped
  (or 12-14 cocktail sausages)

- 1 cup of rice

- 1 white onion, chopped

- 1 red onion, chopped

- 2 bell peppers, sliced

- 3 tbsp of Camping Soul Food Mix seasoning (pg. 25)

- 1 x 700ml bottle of passata

- Olive oil

- Salt and pepper

SERVES APPROX. 4

METHOD OR MADNESS

1 In a heavy-bottomed pot, brown the sausages and chicken in oil.

2 Add the rest of the ingredients and season (leaving aside the rice). Cook until the onions are softening and fragrant.

3 Throw in the rice and pour the water over the mixture (a ratio of 1 cup of rice, to 2-ish cups of water).

4 Bring to boil and then simmer until the rice is cooked.

5 Serve in hearty portions.

♫♩ MUSIC PAIRING
Hank Williams
Jambalaya

HACK

The basic kitchen essentials for most camping trips are: one sharp knife, a pair of barbecue tongs, a spatula, a wooden spoon, a bowl, tinfoil, one pot, a slotted spoon, and jam jars.

Photo: **Jambalaya in our brilliantly versatile heart pot**

Turkey & Ham Salad with a Twist

Not long after Easkey was born, I went out for my first few drinks with friends. As I hadn't been out in a while, the drinks went straight to my head. Giddy and sleep-deprived, I started telling my friends about a salad I had made the week before, and the story was so boring I started nodding off as I was telling it! But in fairness, it was a class salad, and I would like to share it with you all now!

STUFF

- Bag of mixed salad leaves
- 2 ripe pears
- Crumbled blue cheese (optional)
- Handful walnut halves (toasted)
- Handful sesame seeds (toasted)
- 4 turkey slices and 4 ham slices
- Doritos (blue are my favourite)
- 1 finely chopped red onion
- 1 tbsp white wine vinegar
- 2 tsp honey
- 125g Greek yogurt
- Beetroot, cucumber, and tomato (optional extras)

METHOD OR MADNESS

1. Empty the bag of salad leaves on a large platter.

2. Quarter, core, and slice the pears, and roughly chop the walnuts. Scatter the pears, walnuts, and seeds over the salad leaves.

3. Cut the turkey and ham into strips and scatter over the top.

4. To make the dressing, mix the red onion, vinegar, honey, and yogurt together in a small jar, then drizzle over the salad. Crumble a handful of Doritos over just before serving.

HACK

You might not know this, but Doritos, while obviously delicious, also make for great kindling. Place some Doritos where you would normally put your kindling, light it up and unleash your inner fire starter!

♪♫

MUSIC PAIRING
Sam Cooke
Twistin' the Night Away

*Photo: **Beetroot, cucumber & tomato, ready to stir through the Turkey & Ham Salad***

Easy Peasy Mac'n'Cheesy

This is a really simple 3-ingredient Mac'n'Cheese recipe; fantastic for kids and also great for using up the last of a block of cheese. Easkey is a massive Mac'n'Cheese fan. She loves this basic recipe, but if you wanted to soup it up, you could fry bacon lardons until crispy and crunchy and crumble them on top.

STUFF

- 1 litre of dairy milk
- 400g of pasta (macaroni if you have it)
- 200g of cheddar (or any other cheese you have to hand)
- 1 tsp of Camping Soul Food Mix seasoning (pg. 25)

SERVES 4

METHOD OR MADNESS

1 Bring the milk to the boil in a large pot.

2 Reduce the heat to a simmer, add the pasta and cook for about 10 minutes, stirring constantly.

3 Once cooked, sprinkle with the cheese and *Camping Soul Food Mix*. Stir together until the cheese is melted and pasta evenly coated.

HACK

Rainy days can be tough when camping, especially for the kids. One entertainment hack is to get them crafting. Put some macaroni, hand sanitiser (yes, you read correctly), and a few drops of food dye into a freezer bag. Mix it up until all the mac is dyed. Empty it onto kitchen roll to dry. Once dry, let them thread away to their heart's content. Join in yourself, it's very therapeutic and will easily pass a wet afternoon.

♪♫

MUSIC PAIRING
Rufus Thomas
Soul Food

Photo: **The ultimate comfort food, Easy Peasy Mac'n'Cheesy**

Chorizo, Onion, Pepper & Potato Hash

Spanish chorizo is a handy meat to bring camping as it doesn't need to be refrigerated. This recipe is quick and easy to make, the biggest amount of work is in prepping and chopping the veg. It is a great lunch option for a cool day, but will also work as an evening meal.

STUFF

- **400g Spanish chorizo, cut into 1/4 inch rounds**

- **1 green bell pepper, chopped**

- **1/2 yellow, red or orange bell pepper, chopped**

- **1 white onion, chopped**

- **3 small or 2 large potatoes, peeled and cubed**

- **Olive oil**

- **Salt and pepper**

SERVES 4

METHOD OR MADNESS

1 In a heavy-bottomed skillet pan, heat 2 tbsp of olive oil over medium-high heat. Add the potatoes and season with salt and pepper. Fry until golden and cooked through (around 8-10 minutes), sporadically stirring to ensure even browning.

2 Remove the potatoes and cook the sliced chorizo for around 5 minutes in 1 tbsp of olive oil over medium-high heat. Remove chorizo from the pan and set aside, leaving the oil in the pan. Add the peppers and onions to the skillet and season with a pinch of salt and pepper. Cook for 5 minutes, or until softened, stirring occasionally.

3 Reintroduce the cooked potatoes and chorizo to the skillet, and combine with the onions and peppers.

4 Mix everything together and serve.

♪♫
MUSIC PAIRING
Marvin Gaye & Tammi Terrell
The Onion Song

Photo: **Chorizo, Onion, Pepper & Potato Hash**

Wild Garlic Pesto

Some friends arrive with a packet of biscuits, others with a bottle of wine... our pal Pam arrives with freshly made Wild Garlic Pesto, and the recipe! It might be best to make this before you head off on your camping trip, however, if you're on the road you can use a mortar and pestle (or substitute a bowl and a small cup which fits inside the bowl) to crush the leaves and the nuts. The pesto will be coarse and rustic, but will still taste delicious.

STUFF

- **50g fresh wild garlic leaves**
- **25g pine nuts**
- **100-150ml organic olive oil or Irish organic rapeseed oil (depending on what consistency you prefer)**
- **40g grated cheese: parmigiano-reggiano or parmesan (optional)**
- **Sea salt and cracked black pepper**

MAKES A JAR OF PESTO

METHOD OR MADNESS

1 Blitz the nuts and half the oil in a food processor and add in the grated cheese.

2 Add the wild garlic and blitz with the remaining oil to the preferred consistency.

3 Season to taste. It should last comfortably for up to a week if kept somewhere dark and not too warm.

HACK

Clothes pegs. Bring lots of clothes pegs! A clothes peg is the Swiss Army Knife of camping. When you need to keep something out of the way in an awning, or in the tent, a peg is yer only man.

MUSIC PAIRING
Ike & Tina Turner
Somebody (Somewhere) Needs Me

Photo: **Foraging for wild garlic**

Fresh Salsa

Years ago, my friends and I used to have a monthly bookclub. We'd meet at one of our houses, and each bring homemade nibbles and snacks. This salsa dip was my reliable go-to. It is perfect with crisped-up and broken wraps, or a bag of tortilla crisps. It is also a tasty side for fajitas, or almost any meal.

STUFF

- **4 ripe medium tomatoes, finely chopped**

- **1/2 red onion, very finely chopped**

- **1 small garlic clove, very finely chopped**

- **1/2 lime, juiced**

- **1/2 bunch of coriander, roughly chopped**

MAKES SERVING OF SALSA
TO SHARE

METHOD OR MADNESS

1 Combine the tomatoes, red onion, garlic, lime juice, and coriander in a bowl. Stir through and keep cool until ready to serve.

HACK

To ward off midges and other insects, scoop out the lime halves, leaving the centre core-like stem intact. Dry the citrus shells, then pour in oil (any oil you have), filling each shell to just below the top of the stem. Ignite the stem with a match. They will burn for ages, smell lovely, and will (hopefully) keep those pesky insects away.

♪♫
MUSIC PAIRING
Joe Bataan
Subway Joe

Photo: **Fresh Salsa side salad**

Refried Beans

STUFF

- 1 tbsp olive oil
- 1/2 finely chopped white onion
- 1/4 tsp salt
- 2 cloves garlic, pressed or minced (or garlic puree)
- 1/2 tsp chili powder
- 1/4 tsp ground cumin
- 2 x 400g tins pinto beans or black beans, rinsed and drained
- A few splashes of water

OPTIONAL
- Handful fresh coriander
- 1 tbsp lime juice (about half a medium lime), to taste

HACK

Garlic puree makes a really handy camping alternative to fresh garlic.

METHOD OR MADNESS

1 Heat the olive oil in a saucepan over medium heat.

2 Add the onions and salt. Cook until the onions have softened and are turning translucent, stirring occasionally, for about 5 to 8 minutes.

3 Add the garlic, chili powder, and cumin. Cook until fragrant, stirring constantly for about 30 seconds.

4 Add in the drained beans and water. Stir, cover, and cook for 5 minutes.

5 Reduce the heat to low and remove the lid. Use a potato masher or the back of a fork to mash up about half of the beans, until you reach your desired consistency.

6 Continue to cook the beans, uncovered, stirring often, for 3 more minutes.

7 Remove the saucepan from the heat and stir in the coriander and lime juice. If the beans seem dry, add a very small splash of water and stir to combine.

MUSIC PAIRING
The M.V.P.'s
Turnin' My Heartbeat Up

Guacamole

We all know that avocados contain the "good fats". Lots of children like them too, which is great for fussy eaters. If you want to spruce up your avocado, guacamole is one of those versatile side dishes that will go with almost anything you've cooked on the barbecue. If you are limited in ingredients, avocado, onion, and lime (or lemon) juice will give you a simple and tasty guacamole alternative.

STUFF

- **2 ripe avocados**
- **1 lime**
- **6 cherry tomatoes, quartered**
- **Half a red onion**

MAKES SERVING OF
GUACAMOLE TO SHARE

METHOD OR MADNESS

1 Stone and peel the avocados, then tip into a bowl with the other ingredients. Get your child to use a potato masher or fork to mash everything together and spoon into a serving dish.

HACK

You will never appreciate your dishwasher more than when you are camping! Keeping washing up to a minimum is a life goal when you're on the road. Avocado skins make perfect, eco-friendly little biodegradable serving bowls. Use them to present your guacamole, sauces or salsa, and save yourself some washing up time.

MUSIC PAIRING
Eddie Floyd
*Yum Yum Yum
(I Want Some)*

One Pot Potato, Aubergine & Mushroom Curry

This is a really simple vegetarian curry that is quick and cheap to make. It is perfect if you're camping in the colder months, or if you're planning an adventure activity on a day of Irish weather; 4 seasons in one day! My preferred side for this dish is couscous as it is so quick to make on the go, but rice or naan bread work perfectly too.

STUFF

- 1 tbsp rapeseed oil
- 1 white onion, roughly chopped
- 1 large potato, chopped into small chunks
- 1 aubergine, trimmed and chopped into chunks
- 250g button mushrooms
- 2-4 tbsp curry paste
- 150ml vegetable stock
- 400ml coconut milk (OR tinned tomatoes if you prefer tomato-based curries)
- Chopped coriander (optional)

SERVES 4

♫

MUSIC PAIRING
Nolan Chance
Just Like The Weather

METHOD OR MADNESS

1 Heat the oil in a large heavy-bottomed saucepan, add the onion and potato. Cover, then cook over a low heat for 5 mins until the potatoes start to soften.

2 Add aubergine and mushrooms, cook for a few more minutes.

3 Stir in the curry paste, pour over the stock and coconut milk.

4 Bring to the boil, then simmer until the potato is tender.

5 Stir through coriander and serve with couscous, rice or naan bread.

HACK

Coconut oil is a great alternative to butter, especially for sweet food options like pancakes. It can take high heat without burning, and it is multipurpose; you can also use it as lip balm, to rub on dry skin, and to sooth insect bites.

Photo: **Creamy One Pot Potato, Aubergine & Mushroom Curry, ready to serve**

Creamy, Leeky, Mushroomy, Pasta Pesto

If there is one thing that the Buggans' family loves, it's anything with pasta, pesto, mushroom, pine nuts, and leeks. Leeks are perfect if you're not in the mood for chopping onions, but you still want some allium flavour. If you want to make this dish extra-creamy, cook the leaks for longer on a low heat with plenty of butter, then add the mushrooms. The creme fraiche adds a lovely creaminess, but the dish also works well with just the pesto and/or cheese.

STUFF

- 2 chicken breasts, diced
- 250g pasta
- Olive oil
- 150g chestnut mushrooms, sliced
- 1 large leek, finely sliced
- Tbsp of butter
- 150g crème fraîche
- 2-3 large tbsp of pesto (pg. 43)
- 2 tbsp of pine nuts
- Grated parmesan

SERVES 4

MUSIC PAIRING
King Curtis
Memphis Soul Stew

METHOD OR MADNESS

1 If you only have one gas ring or hob, start by cooking the pasta (as per the instructions). Drain and mix with one tbsp of pesto to stop it sticking. Cover with a lid.

2 Next, fry the diced chicken breast on an oiled pan over a medium heat until cooked through. Tip into the pot with the pasta.

3 Heat the butter in the same pan and cook the leeks for a few minutes until soft. Then add the sliced mushrooms and fry for 5 minutes.

4 Tip the leek and mushroom mix into the pot with the chicken and the pasta. Add the remaining pesto, pine nuts, and crème fraîche (if using) and mix until everything is coated.

5 Season to taste, place in serving bowls and top with parmesan. Serve immediately.

Photo: **Creamy Pasta Pesto and view near the Misunderstood Heron, just outside Lenane**

Photos: **Mal & Kiki in the hammock, Mountshannon, County Clare (opposite),
From the hammock to the kayak (above)**

2 Jar Salad

This versatile and practical life hack recipe is from our pal Serena, who has valuable life-saving camping survival skills, whether she is on a mountain hike, or in a field at a festival.

STUFF

- Salad dressing

- Whichever salad items take your fancy

SERVES 1

HACK

A really simple salad dressing that you can make at home before you leave, is four parts olive oil to one part balsamic vinegar, and a pinch of salt and pepper. Just pop it all in a jar and mix by shaking.

METHOD OR MADNESS

1 The first jar is for lettuce leaves, keeping them fresh and crisp.

2 The second jar is where the science of layering salad comes in.

3 Pour a dressing into the second jar, followed by the larger chopped veg; this creates a barrier, preventing the following layer from getting soggy. You can use cucumbers, peppers, carrots, celery, whole cherry tomatoes.

4 The third layer is for semi-permeable ingredients; broccoli, lentils, mushrooms, beans, corn.

5 Next layer is for pure taste; feta cheese, hard boiled eggs, beetroot.

6 Now it's time for the belly fillers; pasta, rice or couscous.

7 Lastly, top with a sprinkle of nuts and/or seeds.

8 When you're ready to tuck in, mix the contents of the two jars together and enjoy the crispy freshness!

MUSIC PAIRING
Major Lance
*Ain't No Soul
(In These
Old Shoes)*

Photo: **Serving up a fresh and crunchy 2 Jar Salad**

Noodle Jar

If you're planning a day trip without the campervan — maybe kayaking or taking the bikes out for a spin — this is the perfect lunch to bring. The noodle jars are a great alternative to soup and sandwiches. Don't forget to bring a fork and a flask of boiling water to heat the noodles.

STUFF

- 1 to 3 tsp curry paste
- 2 tsp soy sauce
- 1/2 jar of veg (fresh or frozen)
- Pre-cooked noodles of your choice
- Spring onion
- Cooked chicken pieces (optional)
- You will also need pint-sized, widemouth glass jars with lids, or other heat-proof containers

SERVES 1

METHOD OR MADNESS

1 Place the paste and soy sauce in the bottom of the jar.

2 Top with filler ingredients; vegetables, chicken, etc.

3 Add the noodles and pack them down so they are fairly compact. It is fine if they stick together, they'll unstick once boiling water is added.

4 To cook: When you're ready to eat, unscrew the lid and pour in enough boiling water to cover the noodles.

5 Place the lid back on and steep; let the soup sit for 2-3 minutes. When cooking, the ingredients should be warmed through and the soup nicely hot.

6 Stir throughly, ensuring that the flavour at the base of the jar is mixed through. Alternatively, you can tip the contents into a bowl and mix there.

7 Eat while hot!

♪♫

MUSIC PAIRING
Brother to Brother
In The Bottle

*Photo: **Heating the noodles with boiling water from the flask***

2 Step Tomato & Bean Soup

My friend Donna has a fantastic cooking blog called **A Cookbook Collection**. A few years ago, when I was working as a personal trainer, I set her a challenge; to come up with a delicious soup recipe with 3 ingredients or less. It had to contain protein, and not require any chopping. I wanted to give my clients a versatile recipe option that was ridiculously easy, healthy, and quick to prepare. She created this. It includes one of your 5-a-day and is packed full of protein from the beans, keeping you fuller for longer. There is no chopping or prepping; as long as you have a hob and a saucepan, you can make it anywhere.

STUFF

- 1 x 400g tin chopped tomatoes
- 1 x 400g tin haricot or cannellini beans
- 400ml hot chicken or veg stock
- 1 tsp onion powder/granules
- 1/2 tsp garlic powder
- 1/2 tsp celery salt (or sea salt)
- 1 tsp dried oregano
- 1 tsp smoked paprika
- Pinch of chilli powder
- 1/2 tsp cracked black pepper

METHOD OR MADNESS

1. Keeping the beans to one side, place everything into a pot, bring to the boil then cover to simmer for 15 minutes.

2. Add the beans and simmer for another 10 minutes.

3. Taste for seasoning and add more spice or salt as needed. Add a pinch of sugar if tomatoes are acidic.

SERVES 2

HACK

I make the soup mix up in advance (celery salt, onion powder, oregano, paprika, and chilli) and store it in a glass herb jar so I don't need to bring all the seasonings separately.

♪♫

MUSIC PAIRING
Eddie Carlton
It Will Be Done

Photo: **Piping hot 2 Step Tomato & Bean Soup**

Quinoa Salad with Spinach Leaves

I know, I know; when you're on your holidays you don't want to think about healthy eating – especially whipping up a meal using an obscure South American grain. However, you might have a day where you need something light and healthy. The spinach in this dish is like a vitamin shot straight into your bloodstream.

STUFF

- 120g quinoa
- 2 large handfuls of fresh baby spinach leaves
- 1 red onion, chopped
- 1 small cucumber, diced
- Dill and chives (fresh or jarred)
- Cherry tomatoes

DRESSING

- Tsp orange juice (fresh or carton)
- 1 tbsp apple cider vinegar
- Sea salt and cracked black pepper
- 2 tsp extra virgin olive oil

SERVES 2

METHOD OR MADNESS

1 Cook the quinoa as per the instructions on the packaging.

2 Season and fluff with a fork.

3 Add the spinach, onion, cucumber, tomato, and herbs, and toss it all together.

4 Put the dressing ingredients in a small jam jar, close the lid, and shake well to mix.

5 Drizzle the salad with the dressing and serve.

HACK

A spinach dip can be a perfect campsite treat. All you need is wilted spinach, sour cream or natural yogurt, cheese, and salt and pepper. Mix together and heat through; it is the perfect dip for toasted bread, nachos or anything else!

♫♪

MUSIC PAIRING
Billy Butler
The Right Track

Photo: **Quinoa Salad with Spinach Leaves, homemade dressing on the side**

Peanut Egg Fried Rice

I have already explained our family's love of eggs. They are one of the most deliciously versatile of foods, and if you have a few eggs, you will always have a meal. Fried rice is one of those dishes that can be made ten times tastier with the addition of fried egg. Throw in some nuts and you're laughing!

STUFF

- 2 free-range eggs, beaten

- 1 red chilli, deseeded and chopped (or half tsp chilli powder)

- 2 tbsp oil (a vegetable based oil is best, but you can use olive oil)

- 150g unsalted peanuts

- Bunch of spring onions, sliced

- 225g basmati rice, cooked

- 100g vegetables (whatever you have handy)

- 2 tbsp soy sauce, plus a dash extra to serve

SERVES 4

METHOD OR MADNESS

1 Mix the eggs, chilli, and seasoning in a bowl. Heat half the oil in a wok or large frying pan over a medium heat. Cook the egg mixture like a pancake, until pale golden. Slide out, roll up, and shred. Set aside.

2 Fry the peanuts in the remaining oil for 2 minutes. Add the spring onions, cook for 1 minute, then add the cooked rice, veg, and soy sauce. Stir-fry until the rice is hot. Serve topped with the egg and drizzled with a dash of soy sauce.

3 Pop in a warm flask to enjoy on your trek.

HACK

It can be hard to eat your five-a-day when camping. Some vegetables are difficult to keep fresh for more than a few days, but tinned or jarred veg work well in stirfry; baby carrots, corn, mushrooms, peas and lots more.

♩♫

MUSIC PAIRING
Jackie Wilson
The Who
Who Song

*Photo: **Peanut Egg Fried Rice***

Tasty Tuna & Tomato Pasta with Capers

Packing tinned food is really handy when camping. It keeps for ages, is simple to prep, and provides lots of culinary options. Tuna is a fantastic source of Vitamin D and iron — and even though many of us camp in the summer months, you can't be guaranteed Vitamin D in Ireland!

STUFF

- 2 tbsp olive oil
- 1 red onion, finely chopped
- 500g cherry tomatoes, halved
- 400g dried pasta
- 1 litre vegetable stock
- 2 x 110g cans tuna in olive oil, drained
- 3 tbsp mascarpone
- 30g parmesan, grated
- 2 heaped tbsp of capers
- 1/2 lemon, zested
- A small bunch parsley, finely chopped (optional)
- Salt and pepper

SERVES 4

♪♫

MUSIC PAIRING
Shirley Ellis
Soul Time

METHOD OR MADNESS

1 On a medium heat, gently fry the onions in oil with a pinch of salt until softened and translucent.

2 Add the pasta, veg stock, and three-quarters of the tomatoes to the pan. Bring to the boil, then reduce to a simmer and cook for 15 mins, uncovered, stirring occasionally.

3 Add the remaining tomatoes and simmer on a medium-high heat for 5 mins, or until the liquid has reduced. Then gently fold through large flakes of tuna, the mascarpone, parmesan, capers, lemon zest, and parsley, with a pinch of salt and black pepper.

4 Place a lid on the pan and leave to sit for 5 minutes before serving.

HACK

When stuck for time, pasta with pesto mixed through (either homemade or jar) makes for a simple and delicious feast. We're all about the low-stress options!

Photo: **A jar of Tuna & Tomato Pasta, ready for the early morning hike**

Veggie Quesadillas

Easkey is a stereotypical 'flexitarian'. She loves the idea of being vegetarian, but also loves sausages and ham sandwiches. I encourage her to eat a variety of veggie dishes to experience different tastes and textures. Legumes and beans can be difficult for kids to get used to, that's why this quesadilla recipe is perfect; the beans are concealed in a little tortilla overcoat. It is also a handy meal to take on an adventure.

STUFF

- **2 x 400g cans of mixed beans**

- **3 tbsp barbecue sauce (use our homemade recipe** (pg. 94)**, or any tomato-based jar sauce)**

- **Small bunch of coriander**

- **140g cheddar, grated**

- **8 flour tortillas**

SERVES 4

HACK

To stop the warm sandwiches from getting soggy, wrap twice in kitchen tissue, then in tinfoil. The tissue will absorb moisture.

MUSIC PAIRING
The 5th Dimension
Stoned Soul Picnic

METHOD OR MADNESS

1 Drain the beans, reserving some of the liquid in a cup. Rinse, and tip the beans into a bowl with a few tablespoons of the liquid from the can, along with barbecue sauce, chopped coriander, and half the grated cheese. Mash everything together with a fork or potato masher.

2 Lay out 4 tortillas and generously spread each one with the cheesy beans (like a thick pizza sauce).

3 Sprinkle the remaining cheese over the top, then sandwich with another tortilla. Use your hands to gently press the layers together.

4 Heat a heavy-bottomed pan on a medium-high heat and griddle each quesadilla for 1-2 minutes on both sides, until the tortillas are golden and charred.

5 Cut the cooked quesadillas into wedges and wrap them in foil to keep warm.

Photo: **Tucking in to a warm Veggie Quesadilla straight off the pan**

Couscous to GoGo

Couscous is definitely one of the handiest grains you can have on hand when camping (although there is a debate about its grain credentials). I love it because it is quick and easy to make. Couscous is fairly bland in taste, but absorbs the flavours and seasoning of whatever you cook or serve it with. It works for any mealtime, sweet or savoury. This recipe takes about 20 minutes to prep and cook, and is perfect when you're in a hurry and only have basics; couscous, trail mix, onion, some meat, and a stock cube. I am not embarrassed to say that this meal has made many an appearance as a "cupboard surprise" over the years.

STUFF

- **250g couscous**

- **400ml of water**

- **1 vegetable stock cube**

- **2 tbsp Camping Soul Food Mix** (pg. 25)

- **Handful chopped fruits/nuts (apricots, cranberries, pecans, cashews)**

- **1/2 a diced red onion (optional)**

- **4 slices cooked turkey**

- **Tbsp olive oil**

- **Salt and pepper**

MUSIC PAIRING
Ella Fitzgerald
Get Ready

METHOD OR MADNESS

1 In a large pot with a lid, bring the water to a boil while dissolving the stock cube.

2 Throw the red onion into the boiling water and cook until the pieces become translucent.

3 Cut the turkey into bite sized pieces and add to the pot, along with the couscous, *Camping Soul Food Mix*, fruit and nuts. (The turkey can be substituted with any meat you have to hand.)

4 Turn the heat off and cover.

5 Wait approximately 10 minutes before fluffing with a fork and gently folding the oil through.

6 Season and serve.

SERVES 4

Photo: **Couscous to GoGo**

Peanut Butter & Pear Crunchy Wrap

Curve ball! Curve ball! This is not your classic meat-and-salad wrap, but a great savoury alternative. It is the perfect brunch-time option; packed full of energy, easy to assemble on the go, and especially great if you're nearing the end of your trip and have fruit and granola to use up. Plus, anything that gets one of the five-a-day into my gang gets a big thumbs up.

STUFF

- **2 wraps (my preference is for wholemeal and seeded, but whatever you fancy)**

- **2 large tbsp peanut butter**

- **1 pear, cored and sliced (keep the skins on, they are full of fibre!)**

- **2-4 tbsp granola (check out our breakfast recipes for a fab granola option** (pg. 13)**, or shop-bought granola will also work perfectly)**

SERVES 2

METHOD OR MADNESS

1 Spread one half of each wrap with peanut butter. I am usually a fan of crunchy peanut butter, but for this recipe I love smooth; there is already plenty of crunch from the granola.

2 Lay the pear slices evenly along the center of each wrap. Sprinkle the granola evenly over top of the pear slices.

3 Roll up the wrap, cut in half and enjoy immediately.

HACK

In Ireland, the weather can change hourly. A good weather-forecasting app or website is essential for planning. We use **yr.no**, a Norwegian weather site that provides an hourly forecast and it is as accurate as predictions can be.

🎵🎶

MUSIC PAIRING
Sam & Dave
Wrap It Up

Protein Balls

I am always on the lookout for simple, no-bake snacks that are healthy and easy to make. These protein balls are a mish-mash of different recipes I have come across over the years. I've combined aspects that I found work best and are the most delicious. The recipe includes cottage cheese, so you will need to keep them somewhere cool. They will last up to 5 days.

STUFF

- **225g ground almonds**
- **225g cottage cheese or ricotta cheese**
- **1 tsp honey**
- **1 tsp cinnamon**
- **100g porridge oats**
- **25g dessicated coconut**
- **50g dried fruit (I use dates) or cacao nibs**

MAKES 18 BALLS

METHOD OR MADNESS

1 Add the cheese, honey, and cinnamon to a bowl and mix until a paste forms.

2 In a separate bowl, stir together the porridge oats, coconut, and dried fruit/cacao nibs.

3 Add the wet ingredients to the dry ingredients and mix until the consistency is malleable.

4 With your hands, form the mixture into approximately 18 balls.

5 Keep refrigerated.

HACK

If your cooler box or electric fridge gets a bit whiffy, porridge can come to the rescue! Place a bowl of dry porridge oats in the cooler/fridge overnight. The oats will help absorb and eradicate any offensive odours.

MUSIC PAIRING
Mable John
Able Mable

Photos: **Kiki soaking up the sunset, Connemara campsite, Renvyle County Galway (opposite),
Mal cooking corn on the barbecue (above)**

Cheese Stuffed Burgers

This is one of the few recipes that we recommend making up and refrigerating 24 hours before you hit the road. They are the ideal "first night barbecue" burgers; once you've set up camp, you won't have to start cooking from scratch, you can sit back and relax into your holiday.

STUFF

- 1.5 tbsp olive oil
- 1 white onion, very finely chopped
- 1 garlic clove, crushed (or 1/2 tsp of garlic puree)
- 4 sprigs of thyme leaves
- 500g lean beef mince (no more than 10% fat)
- 50g fresh breadcrumbs
- 1 free-range egg yolk
- 60g grated mature cheddar
- 60g grated mozzarella
- 4 burger buns
- Optional: Salad items & dressings

SERVES 4

METHOD OR MADNESS

1 Heat the oil in a frying pan over a medium heat. Fry the onion with a pinch of salt until soft and translucent. Add garlic and thyme, cook for 2 mins. Remove from the heat and leave to cool.

2 In a large bowl, massage the mince to tenderise. Add egg yolk, breadcrumbs, and the cooled onion mix. Season generously. Divide into 8 and form flat patties.

3 In a separate bowl, combine the cheddar and mozzarella. Quarter the cheese mixture and use your hands to roll each portion into a disk shape. Make a sandwich of patty, cheese, patty, and seal around the edges. Flatten slightly with the palm of your hand. Cover and chill for at least 30 minutes.

4 On a preheated barbecue, grill the burgers for 4-5 minutes each side until they begin to char. Fill the burger buns with salad and sauces, and top with the cheesy burger. Grab a beer and tuck in!

♪♫ MUSIC PAIRING
Marlena Shaw
California Soul

Photo: **Cheese Stuffed Burgers ready to eat**

Barbecue Turkey Burgers

Let's face it, one of the absolute pleasures of camping is cooking on the barbecue. Food just tastes better when it has that smoky, slightly charred taste. If you've had your fill of beef and pork, these turkey burgers are a great, lean alternative.

STUFF

- **500g turkey mince**
- **1 red onion, finely chopped**
- **1 tbsp chopped coriander**
- **1/2 tsp paprika**
- **85g grated cheddar cheese (plus extra for serving)**
- **Wholemeal pitta breads, or burger buns**
- **2 tomatoes**
- **Salad leaves**
- **Half a cucumber**
- **Ketchup/mayo**

SERVES 4

METHOD OR MADNESS

1 Place the turkey mince into a large bowl with the onion, cheddar, coriander, paprika, and seasoning. Mix well, then shape into 4 evenly sized burgers. Chill for 15 minutes (wrap them up and pop them in the cooler box or fridge).

2 Cook the burgers until golden and cooked through (a few minutes on each side). Turkey dries out quickly so try not to overcook.

3 Heat the pitta pockets (or burger buns) over the barbecue for a few seconds, then sprinkle the grated cheese inside.

4 Serve the burgers in the warm pitta pockets (or buns) with ketchup/mayo and a crunchy side salad.

♪♫
MUSIC PAIRING
Vala Reegan & The Valarons
Fireman

HACK
Always extinguish camp fires completely, and leave no trace.

Photo: **Turkey burgers straight from the barbecue**

Fajita Skewers

Fajitas are one of life's simple pleasures, and they are really simple to make. This recipe is for chicken fajitas, but you could use any meat you have. You can also make a vegetarian option with corn on the cob, mushrooms, halloumi, or anything else you can pierce with a skewer.

STUFF

- **2 limes, plus additional wedges of lime to serve**
- **Camping Soul Food Mix** (pg. 25)
- **1 tsp olive oil**
- **2 garlic cloves, crushed or finely grated**
- **4 chicken breasts**
- **3 mixed bell peppers**
- **1 red onion**
- **Warmed tortillas**
- **Chopped coriander, sour cream or yogurt, and guacamole** (pg. 47) **to serve**
- **The perfect optional sides: Fresh Salsa** (pg. 45) **and Refried Beans** (pg. 46)

🎵🎵
MUSIC PAIRING
Frank Wilson
*I Love You
(Indeed I Do)*

METHOD OR MADNESS

1. To make the marinade, juice both limes into a large bowl. Add the *Camping Soul Food Mix*, olive oil, and garlic, and stir together. Dice the chicken, then mix it through the marinade, and set aside.

2. Deseed and chop the peppers, and halve the onion. With the chicken, thread alternate pieces of each onto your skewers. When you've used all the ingredients, set aside. These can be prepared several hours ahead and chilled.

3. When you're ready to cook the skewers, heat a barbecue or pan. Cook the skewers for 10-12 mins, turning until cooked all the way through. Serve on warmed tortillas with guacamole, sour cream, chopped coriander, and a wedge of lime. Serve with a selection of your favourite sides *(see image)*.

> ### HACK
> If you're using wooden skewers, soak them in water first to avoid them burning on the barbecue.

Photo: **Fajita Skewers, Salsa, Guacamole, and Refried Beans**

Barbecue Salmon & Couscous

Salmon is a fantastic, meaty fish that can take the unpredictable heat of a barbecue. You might also be fortunate enough to be camping in an area that supplies local catch; ocean or freshwater fish.

STUFF

- 4 small skinless salmon fillets
- 160g couscous
- 320ml chicken stock
- Juice of half a lemon
- 40ml extra virgin olive oil
- 80g cherry tomatoes, halved

DRESSING

- 30ml olive oil
- Juice of half a lemon
- 1 tsp honey
- 50g cherry tomatoes, chopped
- 1/2 clove garlic, crushed
- 1 heaped tbsp capers
- 2 tbsp dry basil
- 50g olives, chopped

♪♫
MUSIC PAIRING
Croupier Funk
Recipe

METHOD OR MADNESS

1 Place the couscous in a bowl and pour the boiling stock over the top. Cover with a plate and leave to stand for 5 minutes, then fork through to separate the grains. Mix in lemon juice, olive oil, and tomatoes, season with a pinch of salt and pepper. Set to one side.

2 Lay a flat sheet of foil onto your work surface. Spoon a quarter portion of couscous on to one half, and place the salmon fillet on top. Drizzle with oil. Fold the other half of the foil over to envelope the ingredients, add a splash of water, and press the foil edges tightly to form a seal.

3 Place the foil package over indirect heat, close the lid (if applicable) and cook for 12-14 minutes. While the salmon is cooking whisk the dressing ingredients together in a bowl.

4 Once cooked, tear open the parcels and spoon the dressing over the salmon before serving.

SERVES 4

Photo: **Plated Barbecue Salmon and Couscous on a dry stone wall**

The Mustard Lady's Best Ever Trout

There is a woman called The Mustard Lady who lives in Galway. She makes mustards with amazing combinations, such as Buckie Mustard, Galway Hooker Pale Ale Mustard, Old Engine Oil Mustard... She gave Malachy this Heart-of-Connacht trout recipe (which I'm sure you can substitute with non-Lough Corrib trout – just don't tell her!)

STUFF

- **Trout**

- **Newspaper**

- *(Honestly, this is everything. She doesn't even mention salt... or utensils. Just trust us on this one)*

SERVES 2

HACK

If you're looking for the best mustard any side of the Corrib, check out *The Lodge Barna's* mustard collection.

METHOD OR MADNESS

1 Firstly, the fish needs to be caught on the Corrib, preferably the Upper Lake near Castle Kirk (Castle of the Hens); a stronghold of Grainne Mhaol the pirate queen!

2 The trout has to be what's known as 'a keeper', that is **no less** than 12 inches.

3 By the lakeside, make a circle of stones in which to build your fire. Gut the trout, leaving head and tail, and wrap in heavily soaked newspaper.

4 When the fire has died down, place the wrapped fish in the dying fire and cover with embers.

5 When the newspaper is totally dry, your fish is cooked.

6 Eat directly from the newspaper with your fingers! I guarantee you will have the most memorable meal of your life; those of us who regularly boat and camp on Lough Corrib will vouch for this.

🎵

MUSIC PAIRING
The Staple Sisters
Wade in the Water

Photo: **Gone fishing**

Tomato & Olive Chicken

Pack a jar of olives or two when you go camping, you'll have plenty of opportunities to use them. I suggest black olives for this recipe, but green olives work perfectly too. Cook this dish in the morning, put in a thermos, and enjoy with a crusty bread roll later in the day.

STUFF

- 2 tbsp rapeseed oil
- 2 chicken breasts
- 1 small white onion, thinly sliced
- 2 crushed garlic cloves
- 1 x 400g tin of tomatoes
- 1 tbsp balsamic vinegar
- 10 black olives (approx)
- 300ml chicken stock
- A handful of fresh basil leaves

SERVES 2

HACK

Green olives make a wonderful alternative to capers. They're salty, tart, and very versatile.

♪♫
MUSIC PAIRING
The Supremes
Stoned Love

METHOD OR MADNESS

1 Heat the oil in a large non-stick frying pan, season the chicken and fry for 4-5 mins. Turn the chicken over, add the onion, and cook for another 4-5 mins. Lift the chicken from the pan and set aside.

2 Add the garlic to the onion. Cook until the onions are soft and translucent.

3 Add the tomatoes, balsamic vinegar, olives, and stock, and stir. Season and mix through half the basil leaves.

4 Simmer, stirring frequently, for 7-8 minutes until pulpy.

5 Return the chicken and juices to the pan and gently simmer, covered, for 5 mins or more, to cook the chicken through.

6 Once cooked, shred the chicken in the sauce using two forks, so that it will fit easily in a thermos.

7 Scatter the rest of the basil. Serve with a crusty roll.

Photo: **Tomato & Olive Chicken, bursting with flavour**

Barbecue Fish Tacos

I first heard about fish tacos when my brother came back from the States in the early noughties. He kept enthusiastically referring to "fish tacos at Wahoos" in an over-the-top Californian drawl. I'll be honest, I thought that they sounded horrible! But now I've fallen in love with them. This recipe makes for a light and simple barbecue option.

STUFF

- **4 fresh fish fillets (a firm white fish like cod, haddock, hake, sole)**
- **Camping Soul Food Mix** (pg. 25)
- **12 Taco tortillas (or small wraps)**

DRESSING
- **Sour cream, Salsa** (pg. 45), **and 1 lime (juiced)**

TO SERVE
- **A handful of fresh coriander**
- **Cherry tomatoes**
- **Spring onion**
- **Avocado**
- **1 lime (wedged)**
- **Red cabbage (optional)**

♪♫ MUSIC PAIRING
The Coasters
Smokey Joe's Cafe

METHOD OR MADNESS

1. Slice the fish into thin strips. Make the marinade by whisking together olive oil and the *Camping Soul Food Mix*, and then coat the fish fillets well.

2. Make the dressing by mixing together the sour cream, tomato salsa, and lime juice.

3. Prep your veg: slice the avocado, spring onion, tomatoes, and red cabbage. Cut the lime into wedges and tear the coriander leaves off the stalks. Arrange on a serving platter.

4. Grill the fish on a hot barbecue for a few minutes on each side, until cooked through.

5. Heat the taco tortillas over the barbecue.

6. Assemble the tacos with the veg, fish fillets, and garnish with coriander. Drizzle with dressing and serve with a wedge of lime.

SERVES 4-6

Photo: **Barbecue Fish Tacos with a side of avocado and crunchy red cabbage**

Black Pudding Burgers

Mince meat and black pudding are a great match. Malachy has even started adding black pudding to our Bolognese at home (apologies to the Italians out there)! For these burgers, I use lean mince and very little seasoning, as the black pudding has great fat content and flavour. Our favourite black puddings are **Clonakillty** and **Kelly's of Newport**.

STUFF

- **500g lean mince meat (beef)**

- **280g chubb black pudding** (a chubb is the standard cylinder of pudding)

- **1 small red onion, finely sliced**

- **Burger buns**

- **4 free-range eggs**

- **Olive oil, for frying eggs**

- **Salad items (optional)**

SERVES 4

METHOD OR MADNESS

1 Mix the mince, black pudding, and onion together with clean, wet hands, and shape into 4 burger patties. Cover and chill for 1 hour, so that the mixture becomes firm.

2 On a preheated barbecue, cook for around 8-10 minutes each side. While they are cooking, fry the eggs (with runny yolks if possible). You might need to fry them individually depending on the size of your pan and cooking ring.

3 Once the burgers are cooked, serve on a lightly toast bun, top with a fried egg, and any salad items or sauces you like.

HACK

To stop meat sticking to your fingers when making burger patties (I can't say 'patties' without thinking of *Spongebob*), lightly rub olive oil into your hands, or run under cold water.

MUSIC PAIRING
Bobby Womack
Across 110th St

Photo: **Black Pudding Burger with sides, cooking on a Ridge Monkey Connect Combi set**

Mushroom Risotto

Let's be honest, it is unlikely that you'll be packing a bag of Arborio rice when you have limited space on your camping trip, but this recipe is quite versatile, and will work with either basmati or long grain rice. Our whole Camping Soul Food ethos is to make cooking while camping as easy, adaptable and resourceful as possible.

STUFF

- 2 tbsp olive oil
- 1 white onion, chopped
- 2 garlic cloves, finely chopped
- 225g button mushrooms
- 240g Arborio rice
- 100ml dry white wine
- 1 litre vegetable stock
- 2 tbsp chopped fresh parsley, or 1 tsp jarred parsley
- 25g butter
- Salt and cracked black pepper
- Freshly grated parmesan (or similar hard cheese), to serve

SERVES 4

♪♫
MUSIC PAIRING
Edwin Starr
Time

METHOD OR MADNESS

1 Heat the oil in a large, heavy based saucepan and add the onion and garlic.

2 Fry over a gentle heat for 2-3 min, until softened. Slice and add the mushrooms, frying for a further 2-3 minutes, until lightly browned.

3 Stir in the rice and coat in the oil. Pour in the wine and simmer, continuing to gently mix, until the liquid has been absorbed. Add a ladleful of the stock and simmer, stirring again, until the liquid has absorbed. Continue adding the stock in this way, until all the liquid has been added and the rice is plump and tender.

4 Roughly chop the parsley and mix through the risotto, along with the butter, salt, and freshly ground black pepper.

5 Turn off the heat, put on the lid and leave for 5 minutes.

6 Serve with freshly grated parmesan.

*Photo: **Mushroom Risotto on the go***

Sausage Sandwich with Pesto

Many moons ago, pasta pesto and sausages were the only things we cooked on our first few camping trips. It took us a few spins out to Connemara before we thought of combining the two. When we did, we couldn't believe we hadn't thought of it before. This recipe is fantastic with our homemade pesto, but jarred pesto works perfectly too.

STUFF

- **4 of your favourite sausages, sliced lengthways**
- **2 ciabatta rolls**
- **4 tbsp Wild Garlic Pesto** (pg. 43)
- **1 x 125g ball of mozzarella, sliced**
- **A handful rocket (or other fresh salad leaves)**

SERVES 2

METHOD OR MADNESS

1 Cook the sausages on the barbecue until cooked through (8-10 mins), then set aside.

2 Cut the ciabatta rolls in half and lay on the barbecue to toast, cut-side up. Spread each side generously with pesto.

3 Top each ciabatta half with a mozzarella slice, then barbecue for 2 mins, or until the cheese is melted.

4 Add the sausages and a handful of rocket to your ciabatta sandwich, and enjoy!

♪♫
MUSIC PAIRING
The Marvellos
Something's Burnin'

HACK
Freeze the meat that you don't intend cooking the first night. It will defrost in the cooler box in a day or two, and will keep your beers cold while doing so.

Photo: **Sausage Sandwich with Pesto on the beach**

Barbecue Sauce

Whoever says that hunger is the best sauce has not tasted this one. Make it up before you leave home; make sure you let it cool before you seal it up. When cooking by the fire, lash it on everything and anything.

STUFF

- 1 tbsp rapeseed oil
- 1 white onion, finely chopped
- 400g chopped tomatoes
- 3 garlic cloves, finely chopped
- 85g brown sugar
- 3 tbsp malt vinegar
- 2 tbsp Worcestershire sauce
- 1 tbsp tomato purée

METHOD OR MADNESS

1 Heat oil in a saucepan and add the onion. Cook over a gentle heat for 4-5 mins, until softened.

2 Add the remaining ingredients, season and mix. Bring to the boil, then reduce heat and simmer for 20-30 mins, until thickened.

3 Allow to cool and store in a sealed container for maximum 3 days.

HACK

If you want to make the sauce really smooth, prepare it at home and whizz the mixture in a food processor, or with a hand blender, for a few seconds.

♪♫ MUSIC PAIRING
Marcia Ball
Hot Tamale Baby

Photo: *A side of Barbecue Sauce for dipping*

Anton's Barbecue Marinades

Our friend Anton is the king of barbecues. His Facebook feed regularly contains pictures of mouth-watering bbq meals; from beef joints to succulent chicken, veggie skewers, and corn on the cob. Drool! We asked him for his best marinade pairings, and all his tips are below.

STUFF

BASE MARINADE

- Olive oil
- Garlic
- Paprika
- Balsamic vinegar (or if you can get your hands on balsamic glaze, even better)
- Salt
- Cracked black pepper
- There are no specific quantities, common sense is the way to go. The sauce should have a marinade-y consistency, and the ingredients above form your base.

METHOD OR MADNESS

1 **LAMB:** When barbecuing lamb I add rosemary and honey.

2 **BEEF:** For beef I add parsley and honey, and sometimes curry flakes and or curry powder.

3 **CHICKEN:** For chicken, I just add lemon juice and honey.

HACK

If you don't have time to let your meat marinade, you can still infuse flavour using fresh herbs. Throw a few handfuls of the stems and leaves on the hot coals just before the food is placed on the grill, and be sure to cover the grill (dried herbs won't work). Herbal smoking is best done on a barbecue with a cover and vents to control air intake. It can be done, however, on hibachis and other uncovered grills by placing a large sheet of aluminum foil over the top to confine the smoke.

MUSIC PAIRING
Wendy Rene
Bar-B-Q

Campside Pizza

Pizza and camping aren't natural bedfellows — we often (rightly) think that ovens are an essential part of the pizza making process. However, I came across this alternative online a few years ago and it really hits the spot. Don't be discouraged by the instant yeast, it is easy to work with.

STUFF

- **500g plain flour**
- **1 packet of rapid rise yeast**
- **2 tsp salt**
- **250ml of warm water**
- **Olive oil**
- **Pizza toppings of your choice**

MAKES 2 LARGE PIZZAS

METHOD OR MADNESS

1 In a mixing bowl, add the flour, yeast, and salt, and stir together. Introduce warm water and 2 tablespoons of oil, and mix with a fork until a dough forms. Knead the dough a few times in the bowl until all the ingredients are well mixed. Cover with a damp cloth; let rise for at least 20 minutes.

2 After the dough has risen, turn it out onto a cutting board and divide into two equal pieces.

3 To make the pizza base, spread 1 tablespoon oil into a preheated 10" cast iron skillet or dutch oven. Ensure the skillet is evenly heated. Place one half of dough in the skillet. Carefully press and push the dough towards the edges with your fingers. Drizzle a dash of oil around the edge to prevent sticking.

4 Place the skillet on a grate over your campfire, or on your stove at medium-high heat. Cook for 3-5 minutes, until the dough base begins to turn golden brown.

5 Remove from the heat and flip the base over. Add your toppings, cover the skillet with a lid (or foil) and place back on the heat.

6 Cook for another 3-5 minutes, removing the lid at the end to let the steam escape.

7 Tuck in as you prepare the second campside pizza!

MUSIC PAIRING
Martha Reeves & The Vandellas
Heatwave

Photo: Campside Pizza on a skillet

Barbecue Chicken Pouches

This is another handy recipe that can be made on the barbecue, but isn't actually "barbecue". I know that some of my friends will cry 'sacrilege' when they see pineapple in this recipe, but the sweet and savoury combination is delicious. Also, tinned pineapple is such a handy thing to bring on a camping trip, so I'll stick to my guns!

STUFF

- **4 chicken breasts, diced**
- **450g barbecue sauce** (pg. 94)
- **1 small tin drained pineapple, diced**
- **1 bell pepper (any colour), diced**
- **1 small red onion, diced**

SERVES 4

METHOD OR MADNESS

1 Ensure the barbecue is piping hot.

2 In a medium bowl, toss together the chopped chicken breasts and barbecue sauce until the chicken is fully coated.

3 Divide the chicken pieces, diced pineapple, pepper, and onion evenly among 4 sheets of foil.

4 Bring up 2 sides of foil over chicken so edges meet. Seal the edges tightly; allowing space on for heat circulation and expansion.

5 Cook on the barbecue grill until chicken is cooked through completely (approx 25 mins depending on temperature).

HACK

Tinfoil is a camping essential. We recommend bringing the heavy duty stuff. Don't forget that it can be recycled! Make sure it is washed thoroughly before recyling in the green bin.

MUSIC PAIRING
Tony Clarke
Landslide

Photo: **Barbecue Chicken dished up, ready to serve**

Barbecue Baked Sweet Potatoes

Malachy claims he does not like sweet potatoes, which is strange, because he will happily wolf these down when he thinks he is getting a regular baked potato. These are the perfect companion to our Bob's Beer Can Chicken recipe.

STUFF

- **8 medium sweet potatoes**
- **4 tsp olive oil**
- **Salt**

TOPPINGS

- **Greek yogurt and spring onion**
- **Refried beans** (pg. 46) **and cheddar**
- **Hummus and beetroot**
- **Guacamole** (pg. 47) **and Salsa** (pg. 45)
- **Butter and freshly chopped herbs**
- **Or any other combination that tickles your fancy**

SERVES 4

METHOD OR MADNESS

1 Rub each potato with a little olive oil and salt, pierce a few times with a fork, then wrap in a double layer of foil.

2 As soon as the barbecue coals are glowing red, place the potatoes directly onto the heat. Cook for 15 minutes, turn with tongs, then cook for another 15 mins. Remove one to unwrap and check it is cooked through.

3 Peel back the top of the foil from each potato, split open, and fill with toppings of your choice.

HACK

Bring a Sharpie for writing your name on your food in the communal fridge/freezer, and for playing the folded paper 'Head, Body, Legs' drawing game.

♪♫ MUSIC PAIRING
Booker T & The M.G.'s
My Sweet Potato

*Photo: **The amazing juggler, Kiki The Magnificent***

Poached Salmon with Potato Salad

My dad is a fresh water fisherman, and my grandad and some of my uncles on my mother's side were sea fishermen. Yet, until I was in my late twenties, I was not a fish person. I have a memory somewhere in the back of my mind of being encouraged to try raw salmon in my grandmother's house when I was about five, but I must have imagined it — my grandmother was not a raw-fish-force-feeder! Salmon is probably my favourite oily fish, it is so versatile and easy to cook. This poached recipe is a staple, ideal for a quick and healthy lunch or dinner.

STUFF

- 2 skinless salmon fillets
- 2 carrots, diced
- 1 celery stalk, diced
- 1 small white onion, diced
- 1/2 a lemon, thinly sliced
- Sea salt

SERVES 2

METHOD OR MADNESS

1 In a large, deep pot, add carrots, celery, onion, lemon, 1 teaspoon salt, and 800ml water to make a poaching broth. Bring to a boil; reduce to a simmer, cover, and cook for 8 minutes.

2 Season salmon with salt and gently lower into simmering liquid. Reduce to a very gentle simmer.

3 Cover and cook for about 5 minutes, until the salmon is opaque throughout. Using a wide slotted spoon, carefully remove salmon from liquid.

4 Serve with potato salad, with or without bacon (pg. 29).

🎵🎶
MUSIC PAIRING
Billy Ocean
Red Light
Spells Danger

Photo: **Adding a pinch of seasoning to the Poached Salmon with Potato Salad**

Zingy Salmon Burgers

What really makes these burgers pop is the red curry paste. I love the kick it gives, and it is a great light option for an evening campside meal. The directions below are for frying the burgers, but they will also work on a barbecue. I would recommend oiling the grill a little first, and maybe keeping the burgers separate from the other food in case you have someone that doesn't like a "fishy taste" on their food!

STUFF

- **4 boneless, skinless salmon fillet, chunked**
- **2 tbsp Thai red curry paste**
- **Thumb-size piece fresh root ginger, grated (or jarred ginger)**
- **1 tsp soy sauce**
- **1 tsp Worcestershire sauce**
- **1 bunch coriander, half leaves chopped, half picked**
- **1 tsp rapeseed oil**
- **Lemon wedges, to serve**
- **4 wholemeal buns**

SERVES 4

METHOD OR MADNESS

1 Using a fork, blend the salmon with the curry paste, ginger, soy, Worcestershire, and chopped coriander, getting the mixture as smooth as you can.

2 Tip out the mix and shape into 4 burgers.

3 Heat the oil in a non-stick frying pan, then fry the burgers for 4-5 mins on each side, turning until crisp and cooked through. Alternatively, you could cook the burgers on the barbecue grill.

4 Serve in a fresh wholemeal bun with a side salad.

♪♫
MUSIC PAIRING
The Spinners
Rubberband Man

HACK
Bamboo crockery is a great alternative to ceramic or plastic when you're cooking and eating on the go. Eco-friendly and durable.

Photo: **Zingy Salmon Burger**

Veggie Pull-Apart Grilled Sandwich

This is a great option for when you've had enough of barbecued meat, but you still want something warm from the grill. There are so many filling variations here so feel free to play around. The key is to get a large bread loaf, make an uneven number of quarter-deep slices, and only put fillings in every second slice.

STUFF

- **2 handfuls of button mushrooms, sliced**

- **1 medium red onion, sliced**

- **Large bread loaf (think a crusty french roll but wider)**

- **6 tbsp olive oil (if you don't have a brush to apply the oil, just use your fingers or a tissue)**

- **1 packet of Gouda cheese (as much as you like)**

- **Salt and pepper**

- **Strong tin foil**

SERVES 4
(depending on your bread loaf)

METHOD OR MADNESS

1 In a skillet or pan, toss the sliced mushrooms and onion in olive oil. Sprinkle with salt and pepper. Sauté on low heat for about 20 minutes, stirring regularly.

2 In the meantime, lay out enough foil to generously cover the bread loaf. Brush the foil with oil. Place the bread in the centre and cut an uneven number of 1/2 deep slices (around 11 slices). Brush the inside of each slice with oil.

3 Slice the Gouda evenly and start to assemble your sandwich. In every second cut, place cheese and the mushroom/onion mix, until you get to the end of the bread loaf. Brush the loaf with oil and wrap well in the foil and seal.

4 Place the foil package on the barbecue and heat through for about 10 minutes.

5 Unwrap the foil and pull apart each steaming segment to serve.

🎵🎵
MUSIC PAIRING
Carla Thomas
B-A-B-Y

*Photo: **Piping hot Veggie Pull-Apart Grilled Sandwich***

Lamb Kebabs

I never used to cook lamb, but when Malachy and I went to Morocco on our honeymoon we experienced traditional tagines, and discovered how delicious lamb could be when cooked well. I am working on a fireside lamb tagine for our next book, but for now, these lamb kebabs with a creamy dressing will hit the spot.

METHOD OR MADNESS

1   Combine the marinade ingredients in a large non-metal dish. Add the diced lamb and stir well to coat, then cover and place somewhere cool for about 2 hours.

2   When ready to cook, thread the lamb cubes, peppers, and red onion onto skewers. Season and cook on a preheated barbecue for 3-4 minutes on each side, until lightly charred.

3   To make the dressing, stir the ingredients together and season.

4   Drizzle a little dressing over each lamb skewer.

5   Serve in a wrap, with couscous or rice, a fresh, leafy salad, and extra dressing on the side.

STUFF

- **750g lamb — leg or new season shoulder, well trimmed and cubed by the butcher**
- **Olive oil**
- **1 red and 1 green bell pepper, cut into chunks**
- **1 red onion, cut into wedges**
- **Salt and cracked black pepper**

FOR THE MARINADE
- **'Anton's Lamb Marinade' recipe** (pg. 95)

FOR THE DRESSING
- **1 tbsp finely chopped fresh mint**
- **1 tbsp fresh lemon juice**
- **1 tsp extra-virgin olive oil**
- **1 tsp honey**
- **1/8 tsp ground cumin**
- **1 garlic clove, grated**
- **Salt and pepper**
- **200g Greek yogurt**

♫♫
MUSIC PAIRING
Sandi Sheldon
You're Gonna Make Me Love You

Photo: **Deconstructed Lamb Kebabs; off the skewer, with a couscous side**

Bob's Beer Can Chicken

Bob from **The White Hag Brewery** in Sligo is great craic, the type of lad who will say yes to a mad idea before you've even asked the question. When Mal asked if he had any beer recipes he gave us this gem:

"This is a favourite of ours we discovered during a camping trip along the northern Spanish coast into France... We use a standard Lotus Grill, essentially a small round barbecue with a little fan underneath that heats the embers quickly and consistently. Ideal for camping, but means space is at a premium on the griddle. The beauty of beer can chicken is that it sits upright on the grill, with space for veg and peripherals around it. The downside being you need a kettle grill or other type of lid to capture and retain the heat to cook it thoroughly."

STUFF

- 1 whole chicken

- Mixed spices and herbs — we recommend the Camping Soul Food Mix for this (pg. 25)

- Little Fawn session IPA, *White Hag Brewery*

- Olive or rapeseed oil

- A kettle barbecue

- Plenty of free time

SERVES 4

♪♫
MUSIC PAIRING
**Bobby Allen &
The Exceptions**
Soul Chicken

METHOD OR MADNESS

1 Baste the entire chicken with oil and rub with herbs and spices.

2 Take a session IPA and carefully cut the lid off with a sharp knife or scissors. Carefully work the can into the chicken's neck cavity, keeping the can upright.

3 Place on the barbecue with a double sheet of tin foil between the embers and the chicken, leaving space at the side for the heat to engulf the chicken. Cook for around 60-90 mins, on a medium heat.

4 Voila. Beer can chicken. Sláinte!

- If you're really determined, some of the beer can be used to make a tangy chicken stock gravy.

Photo: **Bob's Beer Can Chicken**

Polaroids from Mountshannon, Co. Clare (clockwise): **Diving board at sunset; Campie at night; Fire breathing Dragon!; Kayaking at dusk.** *Above:* **Marshmallows toasting on an open fire**

Sweet & Savory S'mores

S'more, & s'more, & s'more! Nothing says campfire more than toasting marshmallows and putting them between two chocolate biccies. This sweet treat is Kiki territory, but we also have a "grown up" version here for the more savoury palette.

STUFF

SWEET

- Big marshmallows
- Cadbury caramel chocolate biscuits (or your preferred chocolate biscuit)

SAVOURY

- Savoury crackers (we love Carrs)
- Cheese (Gruyère is our favourite), cut into marshmallow-sized cubes

OPTIONAL

- Sliced meat (salami is perfect)

METHOD OR MADNESS

1 Get the biscuits ready in advance. For the savoury s'more, line two crackers with the sliced meat.

2 Grab your special s'more forks. If you don't have any, a long sturdy twig will also do the trick.

3 Pop your marshmallow or cheese cube into the end of the fork and carefully place over the flames (or close to the coals if you're barbecuing).

4 When melted enough, remove. Place the marshmallow between the two chocolate biscuits/place the cheese cube between crackers lined with salami.

HACK

Indirect heat, constant rotation, and patience. It should take at least twice as long to toast a marshmallow as you think it should, but remove 1 second before you were going to. Don't worry, you'll nail it with practice.

🎵

MUSIC PAIRING
The Astors
Candy

Photo: S'mores over the barbecue

Easkey's Peanut Butter Squares

Mal loves a collaboration, and **Butcher St. Pie Co.** in Galway is one of the best he has ever been involved with. Jess from **Kai**, and Alice from **Rúibín**, make out-of-this-world pies, breads and desserts. Mal expertly pairs their culinary creations with craft beer and music from **The Blue Note**. When he asked them for a one-pot-wonder, suitable for camping, they came up with this cracker for the littlest member of The Girl Gang.

STUFF

- 125g breakfast cereal (crushed)
- 90g chopped peanuts
- 60g maple syrup (or honey)
- 60g Nutshed smooth peanut butter
- 65g muscovado sugar
- 35g butter for the base mixture, and 30g butter for the topping
- 250g chocolate

HACK

Make Overnight Oats infused with the last of the peanut butter. Pour milk into the jar and shake well, then add the rest of the ingredients (pg. 9). Tasty!

♫♫

MUSIC PAIRING
Dusty Springfield
Live It Up

METHOD OR MADNESS

1 Weigh out the cereal and chopped peanuts, and set aside in a bowl.

2 Then get a pot and add your butter, sugar, maple syrup, peanut butter, and place it over a heat.

3 Mix and bring to a soft boil, stirring for 1 minute. Then pour the hot ingredients into the bowl of cereal and peanuts, and mix well.

4 Pat the mixture into a buttered loaf tin and press down firmly.

5 To make the chocolate topping: Wash out your pot, then fill with water and place over the heat. Sit a heat-proof bowl on top. In the bowl, place the remaining butter and the chocolate. Stir gently until the steam melts the chocolate.

6 Pour the chocolate mixture evenly over your nutty cereal mix, make some jazzy fork squiggles, and leave to cool for a few hours.

7 Slice into bite-sized squares, and enjoy with milk or a hot cuppa.

Photo: *Easkey's Peanut Butter Squares*

Campfire Hot Chocolate

Even in the height of summer, Irish evenings can be pretty chilly. Cupping a delicious hot chocolate as the sun sets is always welcome. Just like our S'mores we have a regular version and an adult "grown-up" version, which will warm you twice; once from the hot chocolate, and then from the Tia Maria. Yum!

STUFF

- Mini marshmallows
- A handful of chocolate for grating
- 600ml milk
- 142ml pot double cream

KID'S VERSION
- 100g chopped milk chocolate

ADULT VERSION
- 100g chopped 70% cocoa chocolate
- Tia Maria (to taste)

SERVES 4

METHOD OR MADNESS

1 Pour the milk, double cream, and pieces of chocolate into a pan. Heat gently to melt the chocolate, whisking until smooth.

2 Serve in mugs topped with mini marshmallows and a sprinkle of grated chocolate.

- For the adults, add a few tablespoons of Tia Maria before serving.

♪♫

MUSIC PAIRING
Hot Chocolate
Brother Louie

HACK
Make the kid's version before making your own, or you'll need to clean alcohol from the pot!

Leftover Rice Pudding

When I was younger I never really understood my mother's love of rice pudding. I loved chocolate cake, or ice cream or anything rich that guaranteed to send me into a sugar frenzy (followed by a glucose crash, all within 20 minutes). However, as I got older, my tastes refined. I really started to appreciate the humble rice pud. This recipe is a great option for using up all your rice (basmati and long grain rice will work fine, though I wouldn't try this with wholegrain rice). I use a cup for this recipe, as it's the easiest measurement. Don't forget to stir regularly.

STUFF

- **2 cups cooked long grain rice**

- **2 cups whole milk**
  (you can use a milk substitute but keep in mind that the mixture won't be as creamy, so will take longer to thicken)

- **3 tbsp sugar (any variety)**

- **3 drops vanilla extract (optional)**

- **Pinch of salt**

  TOPPINGS
- **Whipped cream**

- **Cinnamon**

- **Fresh, dried or stewed fruit**

METHOD OR MADNESS

1 In a large saucepan, combine the rice, milk, sugar, and salt.

2 Cook, uncovered, over medium heat for about 20 minutes until the mixture thickens. Stir often.

3 Remove from the heat and stir the vanilla through.

4 After spooning into serving dishes, decorate with whatever toppings tickle your fancy.

SERVES 4

MUSIC PAIRING
**Judy Clay &
William Bell**
Left Over Love

Barbecue Popcorn

In our house, we know it's the weekend when we're sitting around the TV on a Saturday evening, watching a reality talent show or a classic film, with a huge bowl of hob-made popcorn. Easkey still gets a buzz from the sound of the kernels popping against the lid of the pot. It is great to recreate this popping over the campfire, especially when the portable projector is set up for a 'movie night'.

STUFF

- **1 tbsp rapeseed oil, or full fat butter**

- **75g popping corn**

- **Kitchen foil**

  POPCORN FLAVOURINGS
- **Camping Soul Food Mix**
  (pg. 25)

- **Melted butter and salt**

METHOD OR MADNESS

1 Place the oil and the popping corn in a square of kitchen foil about 60 x 35cm in size.

2 Fold into a loose parcel, allowing lots of room for the corn to pop. Seal the edges, and give it a good shake.

3 Place on the coolest part of the barbecue for 5-10 minutes until the popping stops.

4 Tip the popped corn into a bowl and shake with flavour and seasoning as desired.

♪♫
MUSIC PAIRING
James Brown
Mother Popcorn

HACK

Microfibre shower towels are a godsend for camping in Ireland. They dry relatively quickly and are really compact.

Photo: **Film night, using Campie as a screen for the portable projector**

Gabi's Campfire Cocktail

The art of mixology is a craft that was handed down from druids, who gathered around campfires centuries ago. Our pal Gabi is the master of her game, and conjured up this tasty potion for us. It is perfect for evening drinks, sat at the campfire, planning the next day's adventures.

STUFF

- **30ml vodka**
- **30ml lemon Juice**
- **30cm cranberry juice**
- **5 raspberries**
- **Tbsp of sugar**
- **30ml of Jagermeister**
- **A handful of ice**
- **To garnish: sprigs of fresh rosemary, slices of grapefruit and extra rasperries**

METHOD OR MADNESS

1 Muddle 5 raspberries at the bottom of a jam jar with the sugar.

2 Add the rest of your ingredients, bar the Jager, and shake with a handful of ice.

3 Top with ice and garnish with a sprig of rosemary, slice of grapefruit or raspberries.

4 Pour your measure of Jager over the top. Cheers!

HACK

It is unlikely that you will have a spirit measure to hand. With this recipe, the important thing is that the alcohol measures are all equal — a bottle cap or an egg cup makes a perfect alternative. A bag of ice from a local shop will keep for a day in a cooler box, and is the best present to share with the campers next door.

♪♫

MUSIC PAIRING
Gwen McCrae
*Keep The
Fire Burning*

Polaroids: **Fajita prep in the Campie Kitchen; Campfire cocktails; The record bag**

Sage Jargarita & Rum Scaffa No-Ice Cocktail

Beautiful sunsets and evening drinks are perhaps our favourite parts of the camping experience. Pull on a woolly hat when the sun goes down and mix up a drink to enjoy over ghost stories around the campfire.

HACK

To make the botanical, sage-infused tequila, muddle 3 sprigs of sage in a jam jar and fill with a gold tequila.

Shake like feck.

Store in a cool, dark place for around 24 hours to infuse.

Sage Jargarita

STUFF

- **2 caps sage-infused tequila**
- **1 1/2 cap fresh lime juice**
- **1/2 cap Cointreau**
- **Squeeze of agave nectar/honey**

METHOD OR MADNESS

Combine the ingredients in a large ice-filled jam jar. Shake like feck.

Rum Scaffa

STUFF

- **2 capfuls white rum**
- **1 cap Bénédictine herbal liqueur**
- **1 dash Angostura bitters**

METHOD OR MADNESS

A Scaffa is a mixed drink, served at room temperature, often combination of liquor stirred with a dash of bitters.

This one will warm the coldest of cockles. Pour into a glass, stir, serve.

MUSIC PAIRING
Peaches & Herb
Shake Your Groove Thing

*Photo: **Jam jar cocktail, garnished with an edible flower***

Campfire Apple Crumble

One of the golden rules of camping is to only pack what you really need. This recipe was concocted one evening when all we had left was some fruit, some booze, and our homemade granola. We cobbled it together and it tasted delicious; handy and comforting. Over time we refined the recipe and can now whip it up in a few minutes. You can easily substitute apples for pears, apricots, peaches, plums or cherries.

STUFF

- **2-3 apples (sliced into segments)**

- **25g (1 tbsp) butter**

- **1 tsp ground cinnamon**

- **1/2 tsp ground nutmeg**

- **1/2 tsp ground cloves**

- **A slug of Irish whiskey (a few tablespoons, depending on how boozy you want it)**

- **50g (2-3 tbsp) brown sugar**

- **Large handful of granola**

- **Natural/Greek yogurt or cream**

SERVES 4

METHOD OR MADNESS

1 In a heavy-bottomed pot over medium heat, sauté the sliced apples in butter until they begin to soften (about 5 minutes).

2 Add the spices, whiskey, and sugar, and stir. Cook until the sauce thickens and the apples are tender (about 10 minutes).

3 Remove from the heat, divide into bowls and sprinkle the crunchy granola evenly across the top.

4 Serve with a side helping of yogurt or cream.

♪♫
MUSIC PAIRING
Ben E. King
Stand By Me

HACK
If you have any of the apple sauce left over, it tastes fantastic with pork chops or burgers.

*Photo: **Campfire Apple Crumble ready to serve***

99 S'mores

Unfortunately, packing ice cream isn't realistic when camping remotely. When you're on holidays, nowhere near a store or ice cream van, and you get a hankering for a good-old 99, this recipe might sate your desire. It's a fun, campfire-friendly alternative that will satisfy any sweet tooth. It is also another confirmation that there are 101-uses-for-tinfoil, so make sure you pack an extra roll of foil... just in case.

STUFF

- **Ice cream cones**

- **Peanut butter or Nutella**

- **Mini marshmallows**

- **Favourite s'mores topping: nut butter, mini marshmallows, chocolate chips, sliced strawberries, sliced bananas, peanut M&M's, Rolo... go wild!**

METHOD OR MADNESS

1 Coat the inside of your cone with peanut butter or Nutella.

2 Fill with your favorite toppings; chocolate chips and mini marshmallows are a classic combo.

3 Wrap each cone tightly with tinfoil.

4 Heat the cones in their conical tinfoil armour over a campfire for about 3-5 minutes, or until the chocolate and marshmallows have melted, whichever happens first.

HACK

This is Easkey's hack: make sure you use *Askeys* cones. Not only are they a superior cone (in our humble opinion), the name is also only 1 letter removed from the name 'Easkey'. Please don't make us ask-ey you twice!

♫♩
MUSIC PAIRING
Wilson Pickett
Engine Number 9

Photo: **Pink marshmallow 99 S'more**

Photographs: *Vinyl on a dry stone wall, This Is Soul (Atlantic, 1968); shaking jam jar cocktails*

Index

Photo: *Kiki enjoying pasta on a windy and rainy day*

Photo: *Trusty and versatile barbecue utensils*

Photo: **Barbecue Chicken Pouch in foil**

Opposite: **With love from Campie,** *Illustration:* **Zombie Campie by Colacorolla**

Photographs: **No peeking. Head, Body, Legs game gets competitive; Carrie about to take the head off Mal with a Camping Soul Food frisbee**

141

Acknowledgements

Amelia and Julia for their patience, and for making our lockdown idea look so slick.

Oscar and the team at Manuscript Publishers for all the self publishing advice.

Maggie, Luca, and Jonah for s'mores training.

Anton, Bob, Brigid, Donna, Serena, Rosemary, Pamela, and Gabi for sharing recipes and hacks.

Treasa, Eanna, and Heidi for allowing us to shoot in the most magical place.

Irish Socksciety for caricatures, sage advice, sharing our stories and introducing us to Julia, who introduced us to Amelia.

Jess and Alice for sharing their culinary expertise.

All our pals who gave us feedback on the first ebook.

Keith and team 33/45records.com for the help crate digging.

Colin and team Boon for websiting.

Tomek and team Heavyman film for videoing and indiegogo skills.

Lisa and Tobes for letting the world know.

Our regular Camping Pals. Trass, Eoin, Rory, Steffi, Laura, and Cyril for the laughs and for being taste testers.

Pete for keeping Campie on the road.

Photographs: **The family drinking tae; Kiki magically multiplies, Mountshannon, Co. Clare**
Last page: **Gizmo with a Camping Soul Food frisbee**

Notes

Notes

Every saucepan has its lid